Aberdeenshire

COUNCIL

Aberdeenshire Libraries
www.aberdeenshire.gov.uk/libraries
Renewals Hotline 01224 661511

City Safari

Squirrel

Isabel Thomas

Raintree

Raintree is an imprint of Capstone Global Library Limited, a company incorporated in England and Wales having its registered office at 7 Pilgrim Street, London, EC4V 6LB – Registered company number: 6695582

www.raintreepublishers.co.uk
myorders@raintreepublishers.co.uk

Text © Capstone Global Library Limited 2014
First published in hardback in 2014
The moral rights of the proprietor have been asserted.

Edited by Dan Nunn, Rebecca Rissman, and Helen Cox Cannons
Designed by Tim Bond
Original illustrations © Capstone Global Library Ltd 2014
Picture research by Mica Brancic
Production by Helen McCreath
Originated by Capstone Global Library Ltd
Printed and bound in China

ISBN 978 1 406 27128 7
17 16 15 14 13
10 9 8 7 6 5 4 3 2 1

British Library Cataloguing in Publication Data
A full catalogue record for this book is available from the British Library.

Acknowledgements
We would like to thank the following for permission to reproduce photographs: Alamy pp. 11 (© Dizzy), 14 (© David Mabe), 18 (© Thom Moore), 19 (© Richard Newton), 23 den (© Dizzy), 23 loft insulation (© Richard Newton), 23 mate (© Thom Moore); FLPA pp. 9 (David Tipling), 13 (Bill Coster), 15 (Erica Olsen), 17 (Wayne Hutchinson), 21 (S & D & K Maslowski), 23 predator (Wayne Hutchinson); Getty Images p. 4 (Tim Graham); Naturepl.com pp. 6 inset (© Bruno D'Amicis), 6 main & 7 (both © Warwick Sloss), 10 (© Doug Wechsler), 16 (© Rolf Nussbaumer), 20 (© Andrew Cooper), 23 drey (© Doug Wechsler); Shutterstock pp. 5 (© ivvv1975) 6 (© Tom Reichner), 8 (© Yannick FEL), 12 (© Paul Orr), 23 fungi (© James Ac), 23 sense (© S.Cooper Digital).

Front cover photograph of a squirrel reproduced with permission of Shutterstock (© Photomika-com). Back cover photograph of a squirrel having a meal of bird seed reproduced with permission of Shutterstock (© Paul Orr).

We would like to thank Michael Bright for his invaluable help in the preparation of this book.

Every effort has been made to contact copyright holders of material reproduced in this book. Any omissions will be rectified in subsequent printings if notice is given to the publisher.

Warning!

Never touch wild animals or their homes. Some wild animals carry diseases. Scared animals may bite or scratch you. Never hold food for a squirrel to eat. It may bite your finger by mistake.

Note about spotter icon

3

Your eyes, ears, and nose can tell you if a squirrel is nearby. Look for these clues as you read the book, and find out more on page 22.

Contents

Some words are shown in bold, **like this**.
You can find them in the glossary on page 23.

Who has been snapped pinching a picnic?

Grey fur. Short front legs. A bushy tail. It's a grey squirrel!

Pets are not the only animals that live in towns and cities.

red-brown patches

bushy tail

white belly

short front legs

long claws

Many wild animals like to live near people, too.

Come on a city safari. Find out if squirrels are living near you.

Why do squirrels live in towns and cities?

Countryside squirrels live in woodlands with lots of big trees.

It can be hard for squirrels to find food in cold weather.

Towns and cities are warmer than the countryside. There are fewer **predators**.

Parks and gardens are full of tree-top homes and tasty food.

What makes squirrels good at living in towns and cities?

Grey squirrels are not afraid to look for food near people.

If they **sense** danger, they climb to safety quickly.

Squirrels can climb very well.

Their curved claws grip things and their
tails help them to steer as they jump
from place to place.

Where do squirrels rest and sleep?

Grey squirrels spend most of their time in trees.

They use leaves and twigs to build round nests called **dreys**.

They also build **dens** in warm places, such as hollow tree trunks and attics.

These high-up nests and dens are safe places to rest and sleep.

What do squirrels eat?

Squirrels use their eyes and noses to find food on the ground.

Their sharp front teeth can crack open nuts, and nibble twigs and pine cones.

Squirrels also like fruit, seeds, buds, insects, bird eggs, and **fungi**.

They remember where to find tasty food, and visit these favourite places every day.

Why do squirrels like living near people?

Gardens are full of snacks, such as bulbs, fish, fruit, and birdseed.

City squirrels often find more food than they can eat.

Squirrels dig small holes to bury spare nuts and seeds.

They sniff it out in the winter, when there is less food around.

What dangers do squirrels face in towns and cities?

Grey squirrels can damage buildings with their strong teeth.

They can harm trees by tearing off the bark.

Many grey squirrels are trapped by people to stop them from doing damage.

In some places, people also hunt squirrels for food.

When do squirrels have babies?

Most squirrels **mate** twice a year, in May and December.

Look out for males chasing females, making lots of noise!

The female lines a **drey** with soft things, such as moss, grass, paper, or **loft insulation**.

Three or four babies are born in the drey.

Why is it hard to spot a baby squirrel?

The mother squirrel looks after her babies inside the **drey**.

After two months, the babies start to play outside, but they stay near the drey.

This makes it very hard to spot a
baby squirrel.

After three months, the young squirrels
leave and build dreys of their own.

Squirrel spotter's guide

Look back at the sights, sounds, and smells that tell you a squirrel might be nearby. Use these clues to go on your own city safari.

1. Look out for squirrel footprints in mud or snow. Their front feet leave four claw marks and their back feet leave five claw marks.

2. Try spotting a **drey** in winter, when trees have no leaves. The nests are the size of a football.

3. Squirrels are messy eaters. Look for nibbled shells or pine cones at the foot of trees.

4. Squirrels make different noises. Listen out for a clicking "kuk, kuk, kuk" alarm call, and the chattering sounds of males when it is time to **mate**.

Picture glossary

 **den** hidden home of a wild animal

 **drey** squirrel's nest

 **fungi** mushrooms and toadstools

 **loft insulation** material put into the loft of a house, to help keep the house warm

 **mate** when a male and female animal get together to have babies

 **predator** animal that hunts other animals for food

 **sense** find out what is around through sight, hearing, smell, taste, and touch

Find out more

Books

Squirrels (Animals, Animals), Steven Oftinoski (Marshall Cavendish, 2011)

Wild Town, Mike Dilger (A & C Black, 2012)

Websites

animals.nationalgeographic.co.uk/animals/ mammals/squirrel
Find out more about the grey squirrel on this website.

sounds.bl.uk/environment/british-wildlife- recordings/022M-W1CDR0001426-0400V0
Visit this website to listen to the sounds that squirrels make.

Index